Old Fermanagh
Corned Beef
COOKBOOK

LIMITED EDITION

Pat O'Doherty

First Edition
First impression

ISBN 978-1-78073-043-1

©2012 O'Doherty's Fine Meats

Corned Beef™ is a registered Trademark

Photography by Steve Thompson and Elaine Vaughan
www.stevethompsonphotography.co.uk

Designed by April Sky Design, Newtownards
028 9182 7195, www.aprilsky.co.uk

O'Doherty's Fine Meats,
Belmore Street,
Enniskillen,
Co Fermanagh
BT74 6AA

Phone: 0044 28 6632 2152

E-mail: sales@blackbacon.com

Web: www.blackbacon.com

Contents

Acknowledgements

With such a fascinating historical food I am indebted to the following without whose help this publication would never have happened:

The beef farming community of Fermanagh whose dedication to providing grass fed quality beef has been inspirational.

All those who unselfishly provided recipes and tips on cooking: Liz Moore, Joe Kelly, Ronan McManus and Stanley Vaughan. We all know that it's the wee tips that make a big difference!

My customers, family and friends who have had to put up with some outrageous ideas, behaviour and activities during the production and development of the Old Fermanagh Corned Beef.

Belle Isle School of Cookery for the kind use of their premises and equipment.

This book is dedicated
To
My father James O'Doherty

Pat O'Doherty
2012

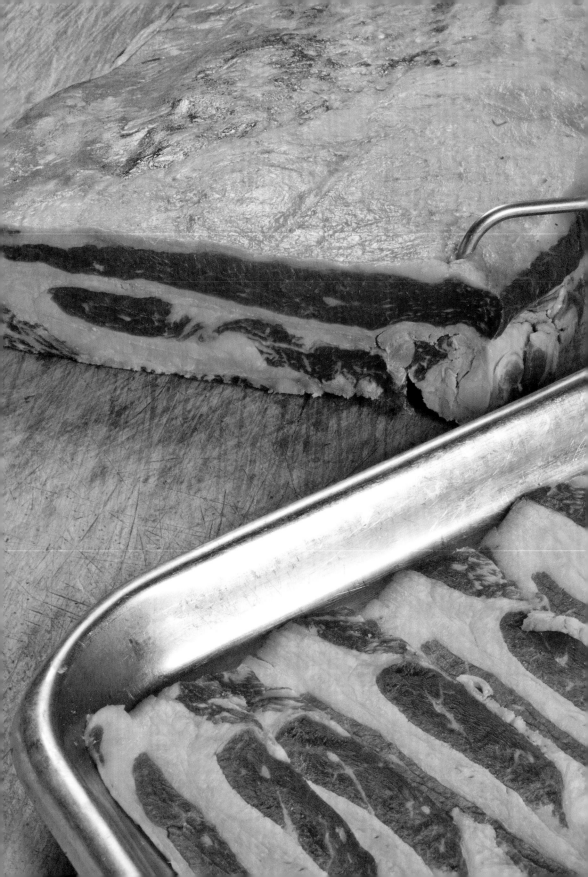

CORNED BEEF
A Lost Tradition

The history of Ireland has been well documented geologically, environmentally and most recently politically.

Ireland has been a country of mystique and folklore. Many stories have captured the historical ebb and flow of traditions. These traditions have imposed and developed their own needs.

Food was an integral part of each culture, and just as some cultures changed or even died out, so too did the foods that sustained them.

One such food that cultural development and modernisation cast aside was old forms of Irish corned beef. The loss of the widespread use of old forms of Irish corned beef was probably one of the most dramatic in modern times.

Although we have testimonies of how old types of bacon were matured, the information on how old forms of corned beef were created is very scarce. We can only surmise that those methods reflected the very basic methods widely used throughout Ireland dating right back to before 1100 AD.

As a starting point of research, and to gain a general opinion of the current attitudes to corned beef, a questionnaire was randomly distributed to 500 people with the simple question:

What is corned beef?

The results were very surprising: 95% of people said that corned beef is something in a tin and is a cheap type of ham.

Wow!… What an overwhelming opinion – this reflects the success of modern day processing technology.

With such an attitude to corned beef, it is understandable that old forms of producing and cooking corned beef have been largely neglected to the benefit of a modern day quick-fix solution.

To understand the importance of corned beef we have to transport ourselves back to Ireland over 600 years ago.

No electricity, no refrigeration, no modern methods of storage … a very basic farming society existed and with it a basic social system.

When farmers killed an animal for beef they could only use a certain amount before the meat went off. So to avoid excessive loss, beef was salted and stored away and, just like bacon, there was a very basic survival reason for salting.

This salted beef in no way resembled the tinned corned beef that so many of us associate with corned beef today.

Corned beef has been traced back over 600 years in Ireland and in ancient writings dating from the year 1100 AD.

In the 12th century poem Aislinge Meic Con Glinne (the Vision of MacConglinne) it is described as a delicacy a king uses to purge himself of the demon of gluttony.

In these very early days cattle were very much a status symbol and, as a result, cattle were only killed when they could no longer provide milk or were unable to work.

As described in this poem corned beef was a rare and and extremely valued dish, considering the status of cattle within Irish culture and the comparatively high value of salt. These very old forms of corned beef and their curing methods were very different to those available today and many people even used a very coarse rock salt (see pages 12-13).

Considering the value of cattle in Ireland throughout the last 1000 years, it is easy to see why bacon production was much more widely undertaken. Pigs were much cheaper to buy, produce and cure. On the other hand cattle were the ultimate status symbol.

In various parts of Ireland various salting methods were used in ancient times. One method in particular is noteworthy. Along coastal areas in west Ireland, seaweed was burned and the burnt seaweed was massaged into the beef and then left to cover it for long periods of time to allow the beef to cure.

It was the vast requirement for corned beef in England that spurred on the increased production of corned beef in Ireland.

The growing population in England demanded to be fed, and corned beef was highly sought after.

Two further historical events generated a huge demand for corned beef:

1. The slave trade

This required huge provisions both for transport to places as far away as the Americas and the Caribbean, and also from the already settled population in these destinations. In fact,

corned beef recipes found in the Caribbean most certainly originated in Ireland and have not only been modified over the last few hundred years but have now evolved into a local Caribbean corned beef reflecting herbs and spices found around the islands.

2. The opening up of the new world in America and Canada and the vast expansion of the British Empire around the globe

Corned beef was the greatest method for nourishing people and its keeping qualities meant that it was highly sought after. Journeys to these far flung destinations would often last for months, so a sustainable source of protein was a real advantage.

Wars

During the many wars all over Europe corned beef from Ireland was used to feed the various armies, not only of England, but also France, Spain and many others.

It was during the Napoleonic Wars that corned beef really became a major factor and it was during these conflicts that a revolution in corned beef itself was about to happen. This revolution would transform not only eating habits in those days but paved the way for modern day processing.

This revolution will be revealed later… but can you guess what it was?

It is exciting to think that when you cook and eat some of the old style corned beef you're being transported back to those battles and the surprising thing is that it largely tasted delicious.

Hundreds of years ago when a farmer killed an animal to feed his family only so much beef could be eaten fresh before it started to spoil. The answer to extend its shelf life was to salt it. Just like bacon and ham were salted in different ways, so too was beef.

In those days salt was not like the refined smooth flowing table salt we are so familiar with, but rather salt with a very coarse rock-like texture was in general use. Quite often in ancient times this rock salt was broken down to cover the meat.

However in more recent times, up to 400 years ago, the most popular size for salting beef was large rounded particles of salt. These particles looked like grains of corn and when spread over the beef the salted beef was given the term **corned beef.**

Expressions were coined, such as: "We are going to *corn the beef*". Corned beef was thus a part of Irish culture.

In today's world this expression is not widely understood because the type of salt used has largely disappeared and the cooking of corned beef is not as widely undertaken.

What is corned beef?

Corned beef is simply fresh beef which has been treated with salts, herbs and spices to extend its shelf life and create excellent tasting beef.

Once the salt has been added to the beef, many natural characteristics of the beef change:

• The first change is that the internal colour of the meat turns to a rich red hue. Much richer and redder than fresh beef.

• The second change is that the texture tightens up and the joint becomes denser. As a result, a joint of corned beef will feel heavier than a similarly sized joint of fresh meat.

• The third change is always surprising: once the corned beef is cooked, it doesn`t turn brown like fresh beef but retains a beautiful rich red wine appearance.

• The fourth change is the delicious flavour, particularly of the fat. It is a totally different food experience to that of red beef.

So just how is corned beef produced?

There are two general methods of creating corned beef:

The first is called the **brining method.**

In this method, salts are dissolved in water to create a saline bath. Into this bath the fresh beef is immersed and it remains there until the salt has penetrated to the centre of the joint – the time it takes to reach the centre is dependant on the thickness of the beef joint. For a thin joint of brisket 3-4 days may be sufficient, for larger joints 3-4 weeks may be required.

In many areas of Ireland local herbs and spices were added to the brine to enrich the flavour of the corned beef. Juniper berries and elderflower berries were widely used due to their prevalence. However, the most potent flavours came by adding combinations of spices and peppers which complimented beef.

The result was a very aromatic beef that was called *spiced beef.*

The second method of corning beef was the **dry rub.**

This method simply requires salts to be rubbed into the surface of the beef. The ingredients penetrate the beef naturally and quite often beef was kept covered for months.

During this period, the texture of the beef is altered, developing a rich full bodied flavour. The flavour reflects not only the salting but also the various herbs and spices added to the salt during the rubbing phase. In coastal areas it was not uncommon to use seaweed as a cover for beef. This itself would impart its own unique flavours.

It is important to realise that corned beef was made from almost every form of beef. It is this diversity that leads to so much fascination. There are so many different corned beef meats to cook and there are even more cooking methods. The cooking potential for the modern day housewife and professional cooking industry is amazing.

Napoleon – what has he started?

In the introduction, reference was made to a food revolution that was ignited during the Napoleonic Wars. Have you worked it out?

At the beginning of the wars Napoleon put up an enormous prize for the person who could invent some method of carrying corned beef long distances so that his troops could survive.

As a result a French scientist developed the very first canned corned beef. His name was Nicholas Appert. Appert was awarded 12,000 francs. In fact the very first corned beef was not in a tin can but in a glass jar sealed air tight…

… It was some thirty years until the actual tin can was developed in England by Peter Durand.

The first canning factory was opened in 1813 in England. These cans were more robust and withstood the rigours of war.

An industry was born…

The funny thing is that it was thirty more years until the tin opener was invented…which leads to some interesting thoughts on how they opened their cans!

As you open your next can, just think – you have a direct link to Napoleon.

War on a global scale was largely responsible for the setting up of vast industries to mass produce tinned corned beef. This expanded into supermarkets during peace time, and today we can go to our local shop and purchase corned beef which may be made in South America!

What a complete transformation in a beef product which founded such a wealth of cooking methods, only to be relegated to the aisles of the supermarket.

The reason for this publication is to demonstrate the vast potential of this forgotten beef product.

CORNED BEEF

A Hidden Gem for Today's Culinary World

The tremendous variety of ancient corned beef methods and products creates a wonderful opportunity for today's chefs

and cooks to embrace.

Corned beef can give new dimensions to many dishes and, with a little thought, new exciting meal ideas can be created.

The following recipes are merely an example of the versatility of this unique meat and embrace the various forms of ancient Irish corned beef types. These include :

- **Corned beef joint**
- **Corned beef steaks**
- **Corned beef diced**
- **Corned beef minced/diced very finely**
- **Dry aged corned beef**
- **Corned beef sausages**

The Recipes

OLD FERMANAGH CORNED BEEF JOINT

INGREDIENTS

1kg corned beef joint

1 small cabbage, washed and sliced

2 small onions, peeled and diced

1 bay leaf

A few black peppercorns

METHOD

Place the corned beef in a large stock pot cover with boiling water, add bayleaf and peppercorns, onion reduce heat and simmer for two hours minimum.

Remove corned beef from water, dry well and spread with some English mustard.

Pop corned beef into the oven for 20 mins @190°C.

As the corned beef goes into the oven pop the cabbage into the water left over and simmer until the cabbage is cooked (approx 25 mins).

Serve the corned beef and cabbage together with other seasonal vegetables.

 Chef's Note The liquid left behind in the saucepan is a great stock to use for a simple gravy. This would top off a wonderful traditional dish.

CORNED BEEF SOUP WITH BARLEY AND VEGETABLES

INGREDIENTS

350g/12oz poached corned beef cubed

1 onion

2 carrots peeled and finely chopped

2 parsnips peeled and finely chopped

2 potatoes peeled and finely chopped

1 stalk of celery chopped

2 leeks finely chopped

Good handful of pearl barley

Olive oil

Butter

2 litres of vegetable/chicken stock

Fresh parsley

Salt and pepper

METHOD

Heat a little olive oil in a large frying pan and cook the onions until just browned.

Add the rest of the vegetables and cook gently for approx 2 mins. Season with salt and pepper. Add the stock and the corned beef cubes, bring to the boil. Reduce heat to a simmer and add the barley. Cook until the vegetables and barley are tender, about 25 mins.

Add some chopped fresh parsley and serve with soda bread.

Chef's Note	Puree the soup if desired and cook the barley in the soup once smooth. Cream or dry sherry can be added for extra flavour. As with many soups a little chilli or lemon zest would also give an added depth of flavour.

CORNED BEEF HOTPOT

INGREDIENTS: SERVES 4

Butter

900g/2lb O'Doherty's corned beef (raw)

2 medium onions sliced

4 carrots peeled and sliced

25g/1oz plain flour

2 tsp Worcestershire sauce

500ml/18 floz chicken stock

2 bay leaves

Salt and pepper to taste

900g/2lb potatoes peeled and sliced

METHOD

Heat oven to 160°C/fan 140°C/gas 3

Heat some butter in a shallow casserole dish, brown the corned beef in batches, remove from the dish.

Fry the onions and carrots in the pan with a little more butter and a pinch of salt and pepper until lightly browned. Sprinkle over the flour, allow to cook for a few minutes, shake over Worcestershire sauce, pour in the stock then bring to the boil. Stir in the corned beef and bay leaves then turn off the heat.

Arrange the sliced potatoes on top of the meat then dot with a little more butter and a tiny pinch of salt. Cover, then place in oven for about 1½ hours until the beef is tender.

Remove lid, brush potatoes with a little more butter then turn the oven up to brown the potatoes, or finish under the grill for 5-8 mins until browned.

CORNED BEEF EGG ROLLS

INGREDIENTS: MAKES 3 ROLLS

>3 pasta sheets
>
>2 free range eggs well beaten
>
>1 tin of Old Fermanagh Corned Beef
>
>1 Chinese cabbage or pak choy, sliced thinly
>
>1 tablespoon soy sauce
>
>Sweet chilli sauce for dipping
>
>½ litre of groundnut oil for frying

METHOD

Oil pan and put on medium heat. Cook the cabbage and carrots for 2 minutes until they are softened but still have a little bite. Add the corned beef and soy sauce and continue to cook for an additional 2 minutes. Set aside to cool completely.

Lay out the fresh pasta sheets and cut them into squares approximately 16cm x 16cm.

Divide the mixture between the sheets and fold each side up to enclose the filling, brush the edges with a beaten egg mix so the edges can stick well.

Dip the pasta parcel into the beaten egg mixture and immediately into a hot pan/wok. Cook for 2 minutes on each side until lightly browned. Remove rolls from the hot oil with a slotted spoon and place on absorbent kitchen towel.

Repeat until all egg rolls are fried.

Serve rolls with a ramekin of sweet chilli sauce.

> **Pat's tip:** This filling can be used in pancakes, crepes, sandwiches or wraps.

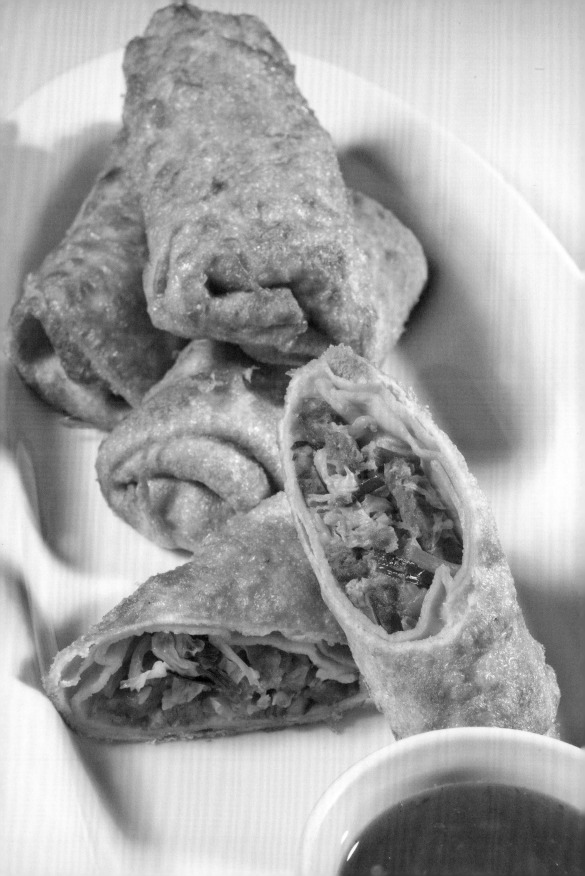

OLD FERMANAGH CORNED BEEF CROQUETTES

INGREDIENTS: SERVES 4

350g /12oz cooked corned beef shredded

350g/12oz mashed potatoes

1 onion finely chopped

1 clove garlic finely chopped

Plain flour for dusting

1 free range egg

60g/2oz breadcrumbs

½ teaspoon thyme leaves

1 tbs flat-leaved parsley finely chopped

1 dash lime juice

1 good splash of Worcestershire sauce

Black pepper to taste

Vegetable oil for frying (preferably rapeseed oil)

Knob of butter

FOR THE PARSLEY SAUCE

400ml/14 floz milk

42g/1½ oz butter

42g/1½ oz flour

120ml/4 floz chicken stock

4 tbsp chopped flat-leaved parsley

Salt and pepper

Freshly ground nutmeg

METHOD

Cook the onions and garlic in butter or oil with a pinch of salt until they begin to soften.

Add this to the shredded corned beef, mashed potatoes, lime juice, Worcestershire sauce, parsley and thyme. Season to taste and stir well.
Mould the corned beef mixture into fat sausage shapes and chill for one hour at least.

Place 3 shallow dishes in front of you. Put the flour in one, eggs in the next and breadcrumbs in the last. Dip each croquettes into each dish, first the flour then coat in the egg mix and finally into the breadcrumbs. This can be done a day in advance and also frozen if required.

To make the parsley sauce melt the butter in a pan until it foams, add the flour and stir well. Reduce the heat and allow the roux to cook through without colouring. Heat the stock and milk together in a pan to a simmer.

Remove the roux from the heat and add the milk and stock to it little by little whisking well in between each addition to avoid lumps.

Return to the heat and keep whisking until it starts to thicken a little. Add the chopped parsley and heat for another 5-10mins.

Season with salt, pepper and nutmeg to taste. Add a little more stock or milk if necessary to adjust thickness of the sauce.

Before serving , heat enough oil in a large frying pan to shallow fry the croquettes. Cook each one until golden brown all over and piping hot in the middle. Serve with plenty of parsley and mashed potatoes.

OLD FERMANAGH CORNED BEEF RAVIOLI WITH SAGE BUTTER

INGREDIENTS: SERVES 4

FOR THE PASTA

> 550g /1lb 2oz strong pasta flour (tip`oo`)
>
> 4 fresh eggs
>
> Salt

FOR THE FILLING:

> 350g /12oz streaky beef bacon chopped into lardons
>
> 1 onion finely sliced
>
> Knob of butter

FOR THE SAGE BUTTER:

> 75g/3oz butter
>
> 12 sage leaves (tablespoon of dried sage if fresh is unavailable)

METHOD

TO MAKE THE PASTA:

Sieve the flour and salt onto a clean surface and make a well in the centre. Break the eggs into the middle of the well and, using a fork, make a circular motion and gradually bring the flour into the middle of the egg. It will come together into a dough quickly.

Now you can start to use your hands. Knead for 5 to 6 minutes until smooth and elastic. Once you have reached this point, wrap the pasta in cling film and place in the fridge to rest for 30 minutes.

TO MAKE THE FILLING:

Cook the onions in butter until soft. Remove.

Fry the corned beef bacon lardons for approx 3 minutes. Remove and mix with the cooked onions. Let mixture cool.

Remove the pasta from the fridge and cut into four. Remove 1 piece at a time (keeping the rest covered in case of drying out). Flatten the pasta slightly and then put it through a pasta machine turning and folding four times to improve elasticity. Gradually take the pasta down to the thinnest level. Once finished repeat for other 3 pieces.

Stamp out pasta shapes with shape of your choice.

Roll 1 teaspoon of corned beef mixture into a ball and place on one half of each pasta disc. Brush the edges with beaten egg or water. Fold the disc in half sealing round the filling to expel any air.

To cook – pop the ravioli into a saucepan of boiling salted water. Reduce heat and poach for 2 minutes. Drain.

SAGE BUTTER:

Melt the butter in a saucepan and add sage leaves and fry until crispy, do not allow the butter to burn. Carefully remove leaves to a plate.

Plate up the ravioli, pour over the juices of saucepan and garnish with crispy sage leaves.

Chef's Note	Any pasta sauce of your liking would work equally as well with this ravioli. Lardons from any style of corned beef would be great.

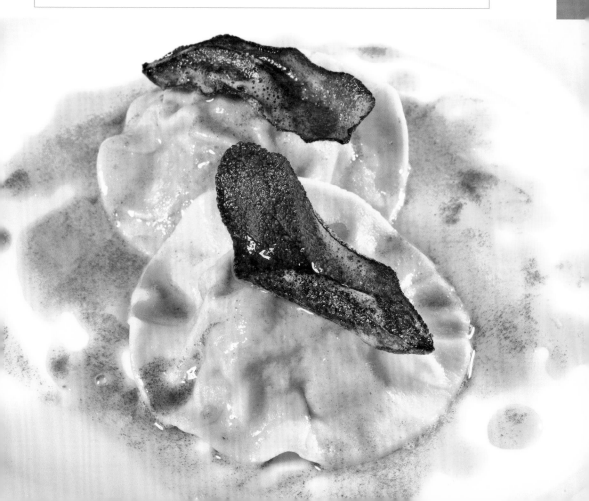

CHINESE STYLE CORNED BEEF PANCAKES

INGREDIENTS:

FOR THE PANCAKES

> 300g plain flour
>
> 1 teaspoon Sesame oil
>
> 100ml boiling water

> **Pat's tip:** the pancakes can be made in advance and are great for starter or main course.

FOR THE STIR FRY:

> 16 thin slices of corned beef preferably with a good fat/lean balance
>
> 2 scallions
>
> 2 red peppers
>
> 1 Chinese cabbage
>
> 300g chestnut mushrooms
>
> 1 tablespoon soy sauce
>
> Groundnut oil
>
> 1 tin cooked black beans
>
> Hoisin sauce for dipping

> **Chef's Note** This has to be one of the quickest and tastiest corned beef teatime treats and the corned beef can be accompanied with other meats if desired.

METHOD

To prepare the pancakes place the flour, sesame oil and the hot water in a food processor. Pulse the ingredients together and remove when a nice smooth dough has formed. Wrap dough in some cling film and rest for 20 minutes.

Once rested remove from clingfilm and divide into 20-24 even pieces. Using a rolling pin, roll each piece out gently on a floured surface until very thin and roughly 16cm circles.

Heat a dry saucepan to a medium heat and lightly dust each pancake before placing it into the pan. Cook each pancake for one minute on each side. Drizzle each pancake with a little sesame oil once removed from the pan. Separate each pancake with a little parchment paper and keep warm in the oven on low heat until ready to serve.

To prepare the stirfry, heat the wok until very hot and add the groundnut oil. Add the chopped corned beef and stirfry for 1 minute until just cooked. Add the vegetables. Stirfry for a further 2 minutes until cooked so that the vegetables still have a little bite to them. Add the soy sauce and black beans to the wok, stir everything together and allow to cook for a further 1 minute until the sauce has thickened.

Serve the corned beef stirfry with a ramekin of Hoisin sauce and 3 pancakes.

OLD FERMANAGH CORNED BEEF CARPACIO WITH BEETROOT SALAD

CORNED BEEF & BEETROOT TERRINE

INGREDIENTS: SERVES 6

- 4 beetroots, cooked and skinned
- 110g/4oz shredded, cooked corned beef
- 1 small red onion
- Handful of mint leaves
- 5 gelatine leaves
- 45ml/1¾ floz white wine vinegar
- 45ml/1¾ floz white balsamic vinegar
- 1 tsp honey
- 45ml/1¾ floz water
- Salt and pepper to taste

TO SERVE:

- 1 tbsp chopped mint leaves
- 2 tbsp lime juice
- 2 tbsp Irish rapeseed oil

METHOD

Line a terrine/2 lb loaf tin or 6 ramekins with baking paper. Chop the onion and mint leaves finely. Cut the beetroot into small cubes or thin rounds. Layer some beetroot at the bottom of the terrine. Follow with a layer of shredded corned beef, chopped onion and then a generous layer of chopped mint. Repeat and finish with a layer of beetroot.

Mix the vinegars, the water, honey and salt and pepper in a small bowl and heat together, until the honey is dissolved. Soften the gelatin leaves in a bowl with cold water, completely covered. Once soft, squeeze the excess water from the leaves and add to the warm vinegar sauce. Stir until completely dissolved.

Pour the warm, runny gelatin over the terrine until covered. Press slightly down, cover and refrigerate until set, at least 6 hours, but preferably overnight or longer for a better flavour.

Mix all the rapeseed oil, lime and mint together and leave to infuse.

Slice the terrine thickly and serve with some mint dressing.

OLD FERMANAGH CORNED BEEF CASSOLET

INGREDIENTS: SERVES 6

6 slices of Old Fermanagh Corned Beef diced

300g smoked corned beef sausages sliced roughly 2cm slices

1 tin of cooked haricot beans

1 celery stick diced

1 small onion diced

1 large carrot diced

6 cloves of garlic crushed and peeled

1 sprig of fresh thyme

1 can of chopped tomatoes

350ml dry white wine

Juice of 1 lemon

2 tbsp olive oil

A handful of fresh parsley, chopped

METHOD

Heat the oven to 120°C.

Heat the olive oil in a deep oven proof dish, add the corned beef and fry on medium heat for approx 2 minutes. Add the celery onion, carrot and garlic and sweat for a further 5 minutes.

Add the tomatoes and thyme and cook for another 5 minutes.

Add the sausages, beans, white wine and pour in 1.2 litres of water. Bring to the boil and add the salt, pepper and lemon juice.

Transfer the casserole to the oven, uncovered for 45 minutes. At the end of this time the beans will be soft and creamy in texture and the juices should have thickened.

Serve with a generous salad and rustic crunchy bread.

OLD FERMANAGH CORNED BEEF IN RICE PAPER

INGREDIENTS:SERVES 4

4-8 rice flour pancakes (easily obtained in your local health food outlet)

50g/2oz cream cheese

450g/1lb thinly sliced cooked corned beef

Fresh parsley chopped

1 fresh red or green chilli, deseeded and finely chopped

2 tsp freshly grated ginger

110g/4oz grated carrot

½ cucumber, peeled with a potato peeler and cut into fine battons

1 handful of mixed salad leaves

2 scallions, cut into fine sticks

FOR THE DIPPING SAUCE

Juice of 1 lime

2 tbsp fresh ginger, finely grated

1 tbsp water

1-2 tsp sugar to taste

> **Pat's tip:** If rice paper is unavailable; remove crusts off white slices of bread. Flatten very thinly with rolling pin and use instead of rice paper. The result is excellent.

METHOD

Fill a large bowl with hot water and dip the pancakes individually into the water until they become soft and pliable, this takes only 20 seconds. Remove the pancakes and lay out flat on a tea towel.

Arrange some salad leaves, carrot and cucumber sticks, a little ginger, chilli, parsley and scallions over the centre of the pancake. Add some sliced corned beef and then top with a spread of cream cheese.

Fold part of the pancake over the filling, seal the sides and roll up neatly and as tightly as you can before the pancake dries out. Chill under a clean damp cloth until needed .

TO MAKE THE DIPPING SAUCE:

Mix all the ingredients together and taste, adjust flavour if required by adding a little salt or pepper, but be careful as this sauce is designed to be quite delicate.

Cut the rolls into 2-3 pieces and serve with drinks or in half to serve as a starter. These are a very delightful light starter to any meal and are excellent also as party food.

CORNED BEEF HASH

INGREDIENTS

> Cooked joint of corned beef
>
> 2 cooked potatoes roughly chopped
>
> Cabbage (already cooked and cooled)
>
> 1 onion chopped
>
> 1 carrot diced
>
> 2 eggs

METHOD

Lightly heat a pan with a drizzle of olive oil. Shred the corned beef with a fork and pop into pan with chopped onions, carrots and cabbage. Stir for a few minutes to get the mixture evenly balanced. Taste and adjust with a little salt and pepper if required.

Once well blended and cooked, place a flat plate on top of the mixture and press gently until the bottom of the mix turns a golden brown and a little crispy. Using another plate quickly flip the hash cake out of the pan and onto the plate. Serve traditionally with a fried egg or two on top.

The main reason why corned beef hash became so popular was that it was a great way to use up joints of corned beef and cabbage that were left over from another meal.

The ingredients would have varied depending on ingredients at hand. Quite often corned beef hash contained lots of potatoes and a host of other greens and herbs to taste. It is such a great way to reduce food waste and can open many delicious meal options. Enjoy.

POTATO CAKES WRAPPED IN CORNED BEEF

INGREDIENTS: SERVES 4

4 slices of corned beef strips

4 potatoes

100ml single cream

50g unsalted butter

2 scallions washed and diced

100g cheddar cheese grated

Salt and black pepper to taste

METHOD

Heat an oven to 180°C.

Boil the potatoes in a saucepan until cooked through but not falling apart. Strain the potatoes through a colander and allow to steam dry for a minute to remove some of the moisture.

In the meantime melt the butter in a saucepan and add the milk, allow to heat. Mash the potatoes with the melted butter and milk until well combined. (Be careful not to chop the potatoes too much as they may turn very rubbery in texture!).

Season the mixture with salt and a little black pepper and gently fold in the scallions and cheddar cheese.

Roll the potato mix into small equal sized cakes and wrap one long slice of corned beef around the edge of each. Use a small cocktail stick to keep the corned beef slice in place during cooking.

Place the corned beef potato cakes on a greased baking sheet and bake in the oven for 25 minutes. Serve with a simple gravy, sauce or simply a tin of baked beans.

> Pat's tip: For a low fat option remove cheese and cream… the cakes will still taste delicious.

OLD FERMANAGH CORNED BEEF CROSTINI AND BRUCHETTA

INGREDIENTS: SERVES 4-6 AS A CROSTINI CANAPE

12 slices of ciabatta bread

6 very thin slices of O'Doherty's dry aged corned beef

1 tbsp Irish rapeseed oil

1 tomato, deseeded and diced

½ red onion finely chopped

Honey for drizzling

Pea shoots or baby leaves for garnishing

METHOD

Grill or toast the bread slices.

Mix the tomato and red onion together. Drizzle with oil. Place 1 tsp of this mixture carefully on each piece of toasted bread.

Tear the corned beef bacon into feathery pieces and drape a few slices lazily over each cristino.

Drizzle each with a little honey and serve before dinner with a sparkling wine.

 Chef's Note Using a larger slice of bread and typical ingredients a delicious corned beef bruchetta can be made so easily.

This bruchetta would be an excellent starter for any meal.

SODA BREAD WITH CORNED BEEF, CHEDDAR AND CHIVES

INGREDIENTS: MAKES 2 MEDIUM LOAVES

675g/1½lb plain white flour

1tsp bread soda

1tsp salt

25g/2oz butter

1tbsp Dijon mustard

110g/4oz cheese such as brie, cheddar or blue. Cut cheese into small cubes.

1 tbsp freshly chopped chives

6 rashers of O'Doherty's corned beef streaky, finely sliced cooked and diced.

568ml/1pt buttermilk

METHOD

Preheat oven to 190°C/375°F/gas 5.

Sieve the flour into the bowl with the salt and bread soda.

Rub in the butter. Stir in the Dijon, cheese, chopped corned beef, and chives.

Add the buttermilk a little at a time – you may need to add a little more depending on the temperature of the flour.

Mix well in. Put the mixture into 2 well buttered 2lb loaf tins.

Bake for 35-40 minutes.

Allow to cool before slicing.

Serve with soups and cold meat platters… especially with more corned beef!

Chef's Note	Using different cheeses will give some truly subtle differences in this bread so don`t be afraid to experiment… a blue or goat's cheese is a real delight.

CORNED BEEF CARPACCIO WITH GOAT'S CHEESE AND SALSA VERDE

INGREDIENTS: SERVES 4

12 slices of O'Doherty's carpaccio style corned beef

110g/4oz crumbly goat's cheese

2 vine tomatoes, deseeded and diced

½ red onion, finely chopped

Pea shoots or baby herbs to garnish

FOR THE SALSA VERDE

25g/1oz fresh white breadcrumbs

1tsp lemon juice or tarragon vinegar

½ small onion finely chopped

40g/1½ oz flat-leaf parsley, very finely chopped

2 tbsp capers finely chopped

2tsp Dijon mustard

150ml/5floz extra virgin olive oil

Salt and pepper

METHOD

Start with the salsa verde. Pour the vinegar over the breadcrumbs and set aside.

Mix together the garlic, parsley and the capers. Add the breadcrumbs and mix well. Stir in the olive oil and beat in the mustard a little at a time. Add salt and pepper to taste.

Lay the carpaccio corned beef slices out flat and roll up loosely. Place, standing upright on the serving plates, three on each.

Mix the chopped onion and tomatoes together.

Divide this mixture between the rolls. Sprinkle some goat's cheese into each one.

Drizzle over the salsa verde just before serving and garnish with pea shoots.

CORNED BEEF AND CAULIFLOWER CASSEROLE

INGREDIENTS: SERVES 6

> 1 head of cauliflower
>
> 500ml milk
>
> 1 bayleaf
>
> 1 sprig of thyme
>
> 1 tsp curry powder
>
> 300g Gruyère cheese
>
> A handful of breadcrumbs
>
> 1 cup of cooked and shredded corned beef

METHOD

Trim the cauliflower florets from the stalk and divide them in half. Trim off the outer skin of the stalk and chop it into pieces. Finely chop the florets in a processor.

Pour half the cauliflower into a saucepan and cover with just enough milk. Add the bay leaf, thyme and curry powder and simmer for 20 minutes.

While the cauliflower puree is simmering blanche the remaining florets in simmering water. Once just cooked remove from water and place in a mixing bowl.

Heat the oven to 200°C.

Remove the cauliflower puree from the heat, remove the bay leaf and thyme sprig. Allow pan to cool slightly.

Pour the warm cauliflower back into the processor and chop to a smooth consistency.

Scrape the cauliflower puree into a mixing bowl with the blanched florets and mix in the shredded corned beef. Season the mixture with salt and pepper and pour everything into a casserole dish.

Top the casserole with grated Gruyère cheese and breadcrumbs. Bake in the oven for 20 minutes until the cheese and breadcrumbs turn a golden brown and the casserole starts bubbling.

Remove the casserole from the oven and allow to cool slightly before serving.

CORNED BEEF STEAK WITH A BRANDY PEPPER SAUCE

INGREDIENTS

2 slices of dry aged corned beef steak 1cm thick each

SAUCE

200ml single cream

A knob of unsalted butter

25ml brandy

1 tsp Dijon mustard

A handful of flat-leaved parsley

METHOD

Lightly coat each corned beef steak in coarsely ground black pepper.

Heat a little olive oil in a frying pan, turn pan up to medium high heat and sear the steaks for 2 minutes on each side. Add a couple of tablespoons of water to the pan and cover immediately to quickly poach the steaks for 3 minutes. Remove the steaks from the pan and place on a warm plate covered.

To prepare the sauce, add the brandy to the same pan and flambé it to remove the alcohol, add the Dijon mustard and the cream and bring to a light simmer stirring constantly.

Reduce the sauce (this should only take 2-3 minutes). Add the parsley and simmer for 30 seconds. Stir in a knob of butter and pour over the steaks.

Serve with seasonal vegetables, potatoes and/or chips to your liking.

This is an excellent sauce for all types of meats and is so easy to make.

Chef's Note	Just remember to keep the black peppers to a very coarse texture and don't grind too fine or the steaks will be too peppery.

THE CLASSIC NEW YORK DELI CORNED BEEF SANDWICH

INGREDIENTS

> 450g/1lb cooked corned beef sliced thinly
>
> 220g/½ lb sauerkraut (pickled cabbage)
>
> 8 slices of rye bread
>
> 110g/¼lb Russian dressing (100g mayonnaise, 1 tablespoon ketchup, chopped chives, salt and pepper)
>
> 4 slices of Swiss Emmental cheese

METHOD

Heat griddle pan or grill.

Make each sandwich using a slice of rye bread, a spread of Russian dressing, some sauerkraut, a stack of six small slices of corned beef, a slice of cheese, a spread of Russian dressing and finally the last slice of rye bread.

Toast the sandwiches for approx 3 minutes or until golden brown and steaming.

If using a griddle pan place something heavy on top of the sandwich as it cooks. This will keep the sandwich together once cooked. A heavy saucepan is ideal.

Serve the New York Sandwich with a little more dressing, a little fresh salad and typically a few onion rings… this is a great treat in New York.

LIGHT SUMMER CORNED BEEF SAUSAGE SALAD

SERVES 4

INGREDIENTS FOR THE CAESAR DRESSING

> 4 anchovies in olive oil
>
> 1 fresh garlic clove
>
> 300ml rapeseed oil
>
> Juice of one lemon
>
> 150g parmesan cheese
>
> Pinch of black pepper

FOR THE SALAD

> Romaine lettuce cut into strips
>
> A handful of crutons
>
> 300g of corned beef sausages

Prepare the dressing by placing the anchovies, garlic, lemon juice, black pepper and parmesan cheese into a food processor and switch on. Slowly drizzle in the rapeseed oil until the ingredients are well combined into a dressing.

Wash and dry the lettuce and toss it with the dressing adding the croutons at the end.

Fry or grill the corned beef sausages and dice into large pieces when still hot.

Sprinkle hot over the salad and serve.

Reserve some extra sausages as they will be needed for extras!

Chef's Note	Any lettuce or salad of your choice will work well here as will sliced pieces of warm corned beef instead of the sausages.

RISOTTO OF CORNED BEEF

INGREDIENTS

1.1 litres/2 pints vegetable stock

2 tablespoons rapeseed oil

2 cloves garlic finely chopped

3 stalks of celery finely chopped

I large onion finely chopped

400g/14oz risotto rice

2 glasses of white wine

110g/4oz butter

10g/4oz parmesan cheese

Salt and coarsely ground black pepper

450g/1lb cooked corned beef diced

6 stalks of asparagus

METHOD

In a pan heat the rapeseed oil and butter, add the onions, garlic and celery and fry on a very low heat for approximately 15 minutes. When the vegetables have softened add the rice and increase the heat.

Lightly fry the rice. After two minutes add the white wine and keep stirring. Once the wine has cooked into the rice add the corned beef and pour in a small amount of the warm vegetable stock. Reduce heat to a very slow simmer. As the stock becomes absorbed into the rice keep adding more stock until each amount has been gently absorbed this should take about 15 minutes. Taste a little rice and cook until it is soft but still has a little bite.

Once just cooked, remove from the heat and add a little butter and parmesan. Stir gently into the risotto. Cover the risotto and cook on gentle heat until the cheese has melted and the texture is deliciously creamy.

Once cooked serve the risotto as soon as possible because it is at its most delicious once cooked.

Serve with a scattering of lightly poached asparagus tips.

CORNED BEEF WITH HORSERADISH AND WHOLEGRAIN MUSTARD GLAZE

INGREDIENTS: SERVES 4

> 1.5kg raw corned beef joint
>
> 200g prepared horseradish
>
> 200g wholegrain mustard
>
> 4 large potatoes, peeled and quartered
>
> 6 cloves of garlic peeled
>
> 200ml cream
>
> 110g/½lb unsalted butter
>
> 2 large onions
>
> 2 bayleaves
>
> Plain flour for dusting
>
> Salt and pepper to taste

METHOD

CORNED BEEF

Place the corned beef and bayleaves in a large heavy bottomed stock pot. Cover with water and bring to the boil. Reduce heat and simmer for 3 hours. While corned beef is simmering prepare the glaze by mixing the horseradish, honey and mustard together and season it with a little salt and pepper.

GARLIC POTATO MASH

Place the cut potatoes in a saucepan with the garlic cloves and cover with water. Bring to the boil and reduce to a good simmer. Continue cooking for approx 12 minutes until the potatoes have just cooked through. Strain the potatoes and garlic and allow to steam dry for a minute or two.

Meanwhile heat the butter and milk in a saucepan until the butter has just melted. Add the potato and garlic, then mash to a smooth consistency. Season and set aside.

Once the corned beef has cooked remove from water and dry off. Spread the glaze lightly over the joint and roast in a hot oven 250°C for 15 minutes. Remove, rest for a few minutes and slice.

Slice and serve with a good helping of potato mash and salad or seasonal vegetables of your choice.

Chef's Note	Garlic is one of the many options for the mashed potatoes. Chopped chives, leek, sundried tomatoes, anchovies and bacon lardons may also be used.

CORNED BEEF COTTAGE PIE

INGREDIENTS: SERVES 8-10

2kg/5lb minced cooked corned beef

Olive oil

Salt and pepper

I small piece of fresh ginger peeled and finely grated

2 sticks celery finely chopped

2 cloves of garlic finely chopped

2 carrots peeled and finely chopped

1 glass of red wine

2 tins of chopped tomatoes

1tbsp soy sauce

1.2 litres/2 pints of chicken stock

10 medium potatoes, mashed with butter and cream

METHOD

Heat a little olive oil in a large pan and sauté the onions, celery and carrots gently for a few minutes. Season and add the minced corned beef. Add the garlic and the ginger.

Stir well and then add the wine, soy sauce and tomatoes. Stir well and bring to the boil.

Reduce to a simmer and cook gently until the sauce has reduced and meat is tender. This will take about ½ -2 hours. (Alternatively transfer the meat mixture to an oven proof dish and cover with foil. Cook for 2 hours at 160°C/325°F/gas 3.)

Pour the tender meat into an oven proof dish. Spoon the potato on top, this is easier to do if the potato is still warm. Use a fork to fluff up the top to make the most of the crispy bits once out of the oven! Place in the oven at 180°C/350°F/gas 4 for 20 minutes.

Chef's Note	This dish will freeze well for up to 3 months. Try adding a little chilli or lemon zest for enhanced flavour.

CORNED BEEF ROSE

My friend Stan's corned beef with figs and goat's cheese

INGREDIENTS

4 long slices of old Fermanagh corned beef

4 ripe figs

60g goat's cheese

2 tablespoons of honey

Ground black pepper

Olive oil

1 tablespoon of freshly chopped parsley

4 cocktail sticks

METHOD

Preheat oven to 190°C.

Take each fig and make two cuts on the top. The cuts should be a cross shape. Tease open gently to make rose shaped petals.

Take a slice of corned beef and wrap around each fig using a cocktail stick to keep in place.

Slice goat's cheese and place each slice in the centre of each fig.

Drizzle each rose with olive oil and a dusting of freshly ground black pepper.

Drizzle honey equally into the centre of each rose.

Place the four roses on a non-stick oven proof dish and bake in the preheated oven for 8-10 minutes or until the cheese starts to bubble and brown.

Serve with the freshly chopped parsley.

O'DOHERTY'S OLD FERMANAGH CORNED BEEF AND TRUFFLE RAVIOLI ON A BED OF FRESH KALE LEAVES

Ronan McManus's corned beef dish

INGREDIENTS: SERVES 8

FOR THE PASTA:

> 4 cups all-purpose flour
> 5 eggs lightly beaten
> Dash of olive oil

FOR THE FILLING:

> 1½ lbs of Old Fermanagh Corned Beef
> 1 bottle of Guinness
> A few peppercorns
> English mustard

TO MAKE THE FILLING:

Bring a saucepan of water to the boil. Add 1 bottle of Guinness and a few peppercorns.

Poach the corned beef in this liquid for 2 hours minimum. Probe with a fork and when almost tender remove, dry off and spread with English mustard.

Finish in the oven @200°C for approx 20 mins. Allow to cool and then shred with a fork… this should be very easy if the corned beef is cooked long enough.

TO MAKE THE PASTA:

Sieve the flour into a large bowl. Make a well in the centre. Pour the beaten eggs and the olive oil into the centre to begin incorporating the flour. Do this until it is all well mixed. Finish kneading by hand adding more flour if needed for a smooth consistency.

Divide the pasta in half and roll out each half or feed through a pasta roller until very thin. Roll out as many sheets of pasta as possible.

TO MAKE THE RAVIOLIS:

Prepare a smooth floured surface, lay out the pasta.

Divide the shredded corned beef into 24 equal sized small portions and place these portions two inches apart on one sheet of pasta. Place a thinly grated piece of black truffle on each portion.

Brush a beaten egg on the pasta around the clumps of corned beef and truffle.

Place another sheet of pasta over the mounds and press gently down to allow the top and bottom pasta to stick together.

Cut out the individual ravioli and refrigerate.

TO COOK :

Bring a large pot of lightly salted water to a gentle simmer, add the ravioli and poach for approx 6 minutes. Drain well in a colander.

TO SERVE :

Place three Ravioli on a bed of lightly steamed young kale leaves. Sprinkle with Gruyère cheese and drizzle with truffle oil. Add a twist of freshly ground black pepper and lightly sprinkle with chopped chives. Enjoy!